S0-BDO-926

Copyright © 2014 by Woof!))) Media LLC. All rights reserved
Published by Woof!))) Media LLC
ISBN 978-0-9842908-1-9
The Brew Dogs of Colorado II

No part of this book may be reproduced or transmitted in any form or by any means, electronic or mechanical, including photocopying, recording or by an information storage and retrieval system—except by a reviewer who may quote brief passages in a review to be printed in a magazine, newspaper, internet blog or similar site ---without permission in writing from the publisher. For information, please contact Woof!))) Media, LLC, 731 N. Tejon Street, Colorado Springs, CO 80903.

Editors: Brian Bennett and Becky Bennett
Graphic design services provided by Kristy Kensinger, Randono Designs
Cover Design: Becky Bennett
Photo Editing: Becky Bennett
Photography by: Lauren Olson, Kristen Olson, Becky Bennett, Brian Bennett, Tory Rust, Emily Wagner, Lucean Oprea, Evan Simon
Copywriting: Brian Bennett
Proofreading by Scott Asper, and Vivian Morales

Printed in the United States on acid free paper, with soy-based inks. This book is also lead free, and complies with the Consumer Product Safety Act of 2008.

The BrewDogs of Colorado II

Dogs, Beer, Colorado. . . It doesn't get much better!®

Dogs, Beer, Colorado... It doesn't get much better!®
www.BrewDogsBook.com

The BrewDogs of Colorado II

by

Becky Bennett

Brian Bennett

Lauren Olson

Kristen Olson

Woof !))) Media LLC

Foreword

A few things have changed since I wrote the foreword to The BrewDogs of Colorado four years ago. While I had been a long time dog owner, I didn't have one during that time as Denver's Mayor. Happily, I now have a dog since adopting Schuyler Colfax (Skye). I also have a new job as Colorado's Governor. Some things have not changed though. Coloradoans love their dogs, and they love their beer.

Skye was rescued from the streets of Greeley as part of a wonderful rescue program administered by the Colorado State University School of Veterinary Medicine, arguably the best vet school in the county (and therefore likely the world). We then put her into a four week training program at the state penitentiary at Sterling Colorado Correctional Industries, one of many innovative programs through which inmates receive job-training, in this case how to be dog trainers. And it works!

I welcome the opportunity to introduce The BrewDogs of Colorado II, a photographic tribute to that special relationship between Colorado's craft brewers and their dogs. Brewers share a special bond with their canine companions. I know I did with my dog Holiday, in 1988 during those many long hours when my partners and I started Wynkoop Brewing Company, Colorado's first brewpub.

The authors seem to have struck a cultural chord with many of us. Their popular trademarked slogan, "Dogs, Beer, Colorado, it doesn't get much better®," resonates in the craft beer community, and after thinking about it, I agree. Here's why:

We have a national reputation as one of the most dog friendly states in the country. Several Colorado cities consistently appear at or near the top in national rankings. We also have nearly 250 rescue organizations in the state, whose volunteers tirelessly work to find "forever homes" for abused and abandoned pets. According to the authors, a large percentage of the dogs in this second edition have been rescued and adopted through these great organizations.

It is difficult to escape the fact that Colorado's beers are among the finest in the world. They have the medals to prove it. Colorado's brewing industry occupies a prominent national and international position of leadership in both innovation and quality. Who could have predicted that just 25 years after we opened Wynkoop, that the number of Colorado craft breweries would be approaching 200?

And finally, we get to live in this great State. It really doesn't get much better.

I invite you to enjoy the BrewDogs of Colorado II. Just as in the first book, you will meet some great dogs, enjoy some entertaining stories, and learn more about our State and its thriving beer culture. Get a glass of your favorite malted beverage and get ready to laugh, or cry, but most of all enjoy.

Cheers,

John Hickenlooper
Colorado's Governor

Introduction

Thanks to a warm reception from craft beer fans and dog lovers throughout Colorado and across the country, we are excited to share more BrewDogs with you in this second edition: The BrewDogs of Colorado II. Since the original book was released in late 2009 we have come to appreciate more deeply the passions we have for our dogs.

Again, it was a family project, with Kristen initiating the first outreach to announce the project to a list of brewers that approached 200. By comparison in 2009 there were less than 100 craft brewers in the state. Kristen also helped with the photography and you will see some of her work in the book.

Lauren, who moved to Oklahoma City in late spring, took the lead after the initial brewer contacts and acted as our scheduling manager, booking photo shoots and planning photo road trips. She also returned to Colorado to help with photography on two occasions during the summer.

Becky has been a determined and tireless photo and text editor. Brian has been the copywriter and business organizer. Both Becky and Brian also toured the state with a camera to meet and photograph some of the new BrewDogs.

We should note that the BrewDogs of Colorado have their own spread in the book which features their BrewDog, Baxter. While we are not brewing beer yet, we always get the question, where's your beer? Maybe someday we will have some. Right now though, we are the brewery brand with no beer.

This edition features 63 dogs from thirty six Colorado breweries. Twenty two did not exist when the original book was published. You will also encounter some surprises in the middle of the book. One thing we do know is that the emotional bond between us and our animal companions is unique. They don't care if your beer won a medal, if you closed a deal, or if the Denver Broncos go to the Super Bowl. All they care about is you, and they wait all day until they can tell you in their own special way, welcome home.

Enjoy The BrewDogs of Colorado II!

Contents

Contents

Sprocket

Characters brewing beer with character since 1995

On site restaurant built from repurposed shipping containers

In 2012,"Steel Toe Stout" won Gold at GABF and World Beer Cup

Sprocket

Excellent Adventure: Tubing the San Juan River wearing a special life jacket

Annoying Habit: Flatulence and snoring

Favorite Toy: Soccer ball. . . too big to bite so he can play with it for hours

Bad boy of the dog park. . . but rehab is helping. Sprocket's anger management trainer says he can now return to the playground. Abandoned in Southern California, this little guy had to be tough to survive. Owner Melissa Dunn, who joined SKA's tasting room after working as a construction welder says, "he wandered onto our jobsite about 10 years ago, hungry and alone. I rescued him and we have been friends ever since."

A self described "motorcycle mama" since age 18, Melissa named him "Sprocket" (after motorcycle parts, of course) and he has been riding with her for years. Like most dogs, Sprocket loves his walks and car rides, but he really gets stoked for a motorcycle ride with Melissa.

Next time you see a blond riding a black and chrome Harley Davidson, check it out. .. it might be Melissa and Sprocket.

Sprocket, Age 10 Boston Terrier   Owner: Melissa Dunn

EOS

Founded March 2006

Building was originally a bank

"Valle Caliente" Mexican Style Lager won Silver Medal at Colorado State Fair

EOS

Favorite Pastime: Running marathons-has won several dog running awards

Favorite Hangout: Andrew's car

Most Excellent Adventure: Successfully evaded two animal control officers in a chase down Main Street in Moab, Utah

A real Houdini, EOS escapes from anywhere! "I can't leave home without her, she has to be with me," says head brewer Andrew Klair. She can open just about any kind of door. Levers are easy, door knobs a little more difficult.

Andrew came back to his hotel room one evening to find EOS sitting in the hallway waiting for him to return. Baffled, Andrew reenacted the circumstances, and peeked around the corner to see how the stunt had been performed. EOS clamped down on the door knob with his teeth, turned it, backed up and pulled the door open...Ta-Dah! EOS escaped from a garage once by jumping up, pushing the button and opening the door.

EOS, Age 3 German Shepherd   Owner: Andrew Klair

Stanley

ROCKY MOUNTAIN BREWERY
COLORADO SPRINGS

Opened June 2008

2012 World Beer Cup Gold for "Eat a Peach" and Silver for "Da Yoopers" cherry beer.

Over 135 beer recipes brewed and sold annually

"**His ears were bigger than his body at seven weeks,**" said head brewer Nick Hilborn, "and then they kept growing in proportion to his head." Bassets are scent hounds and Stanley is no exception. He lives for new smells, and the scent of the household trash bins are his favorite. Nick now keeps the bins on a cinder block and bolted into the wall. Breweries have interesting smells so for this BrewDog that's why coming to work with Nick is so much fun.

Stanley

Best Trick: Sits and sings with sirens

Favorite Time Of Year: Oktoberfest, he can sing along with accordions in the polka bands

Favorite Toy: Squeaky Santa he's had since he was a puppy, he's a believer

6

Stanley, Age 9 1/2, French Basset Hound   Owner: Nick Hilborn

Yeti

Yeti

Favorite Toy: Frisbee!

Annoying Habit: Escapes from his kennel; smart enough to unlock the door

Naughtiest Deed: Uprooted a large house plant, scattered the contents and ate the plant

LEFT HAND BREWING COMPANY
LONGMONT

Opened 1994

2013 GABF Gold Medal: Milk Stout

Named for Arapahoe Indian Chief "Niwot" which means left hand

"**He was at a sorority party** while we were searching for him" said Wes Roberson, brewer at Left Hand Brewing. "We have an enclosed courtyard at our Boulder apartment so our dogs can play off leash. I realized that Yeti was missing so we started searching for him," Wes explained. Yeti is the kind of dog that if you don't take him out for a walk or a run, he will just go by himself. "It's form of protest," Wes says, "so when a call came in from the girl at the Delta Gamma house, I wasn't surprised." Since then, Yeti has been bugging Wes to rent the movie, Animal House.

Yeti, Age 1 1/2, Miniature Australian Shepherd   Owner: Wes Roberson

Lucky

Brewed first batch of beer in basement of the Oskar Blues Restaurant Lyons in 1998

2013 Craft Brewery of the Year, Beverage World

First craft brewery to can; began with Dale's Pale Ale

The puppy survived two days in the tornado rubble, so "Lucky is her name." She and her littermates were just four weeks old when the tornadoes ripped through Alabama in April of 2011. Oskar Blues brewer Lauren Wiersma painfully recalls, "My best friend was killed in the storms so I volunteered to help. I found this little puppy in the rubble and adopted her."

Lucky has always been pretty hyperactive, so Lauren enrolled her into doggie boot camp. A week of overnight immersion training with minimal owner interaction, was the plan. "She needs another week," the school said. She eventually flunked out because she was a bad influence on the other dogs!

Once, when Lucky escaped and ran away from home, Lauren's friends helped lure her back by the smell of cooking bacon!

Lucky

Favorite Toy: Kong, but she gets mad at it because it takes crazy bounces

Naughtiest Deed: She eats underwear; pink panties by Victoria's Secret

Mischievous Act: Got into garden and ate the tomatoes and chilies

Lucky, Age 2 1/2, German Shorthair Pointer / Rat Terrier mix   Owner: Lauren Wiersma   11

Animal & Snuffy

Animal & Snuffy

Favorite Food/Treat: Toothpaste

Best Trick: Still working on "sit" and "stay"

Favorite Pastime: Playing at the brewery

Opened May 2011

Beers are named for Pikes Peak Regional landmarks

Gold Medal 2013 Colorado State Fair "Penrose Private Reserve"

What do Labradoodles and the Muppets have in common? Pikes Peak Brewing Company of course! When brewery owner Chris lost his beloved "BrewDog" shortly after the brewery opened in 2011, it was awhile before he decided to add a new member to the Wright family. It was his daughters, Natalie and Lydia, who talked him into adopting a puppy. "We went to choose one, and came home with a pair-one for each girl!" says Chris. The girls named the fluffy, bouncy pair after the Muppet's wild drummer, Animal and Big Bird's friend, Snuffy. Time will tell if their personalities resemble their namesakes!

Two puppies and two little girls are a great combination of love and family fun...and Chris has double BrewDogs!

Animal & Snuffy, Age 4 months, Labradoodle Owner: Chris Wright

Galileo (Gali)

Loveland's First Brewery, 2010

Focus on German Style Lagers and Ales

GABF Bronze for Little Red Cap 2012

Galileo

Favorite Toy: Tennis balls, he hoards them and does not share

Naughtiest Deed: Picks fights with other dogs

Demeanor: Aloof and calm.

He's a playmate and a protector for brewery owner Don Chapman's little girls, aged two and four. These girls are lucky to have Galileo (Gali) as their pal. Wherever they go, he is right there. Don and his wife adopted Gali at the Cedaredge Apple Festival from the local shelter who had a booth there. "He was probably a ranch dog, and seemed well cared for," said Don.

When the girls (Inara, 4, and Elsa 2) came he was in his element. If one strays too far away he shepherds her back. Camping trips with the family are less stressful when you have Gali along. No one ever strays too far into the woods. At home he is always watchful and at night he sleeps at the foot of their bed.

Galileo (Gali), Age 10, Australian Shepherd   Owner: Don Chapman

Honey

In a Opened July 4, 2012

People's Choice Gnarly Barley

Occupy a century old building in downtown Loveland

"**She fetched a ball once** when we met her at the Weld County Humane Society. We took her home and after all these years she hasn't fetched since," said Kari Klapper co-owner of Loveland Ale Works. She's not shy about helping herself in the kitchen, though. "She will steal food from the counter as we are standing there," says Nick Callaway, Kari's husband and brewery partner, "in fact she once ate an entire piping hot casserole without making a sound."

Since their baby arrived, Honey has become a loving, loyal family protector often snuggling with the baby during naps.

Honey

Favorite Toy: Baby's stuffed animals

Excellent Adventure: Lost for 5 hours in Chatfield Park

Annoying Habit: 'Chow-hound'...steals food

Honey, Age 10, Chow Mix   Owners: Nick Callaway and Kari Klapper

Otis Mae

Otis Mae

Favorite Pastime: Walks. . .short walks, because bulldogs have short legs

Favorite Treat: Homemade peanut butter and bacon treats... yumm

Most Excellent Adventure: Escaped from the back yard to sit in the front yard

BRISTOL BREWING COMPANY
COLORADO SPRINGS

Founded 1994

Laughing Lab Scottish Ale is the most decorated beer at the GABF (9 Medals)

In 2013, renovated and moved into an historical schoolhouse called Ivywild School

She hasn't licked the chrome off a bumper. . .yet. If you are an English Bulldog you have a tongue built for some serious "lickin'." Lynne Blesener, Bristol's most tenured employee, doesn't need a morning alarm clock because Otis just gives her face big sloppy kisses. There is a downside to the licking habit though; she once

licked all the fabric off a sofa. It tasted so good she decided to have more, and chewed up the whole thing! When Lynne came home the stuffing was all over the house!

Otis Mae, like lots of girls, is a shoe hound. Lynne sometimes comes to work wearing mismatched shoes because Otis steals and hides them in the backyard. She doesn't seem to have preference for right or left.

Otis Mae, Age 7, English Bulldog Owner: Lynne Blesener

Rocco & Buddy

Opened December 2012

The 11th brewery to open in Fort Collins

Owner Sean Nook still home brews and produces instructional video

These little dogs like climbing . . . not necessarily onto your lap, but up rocks and steep mountain trails. Buddy had experienced some tough times before Sean Nook, owner and operator of Black Bottle Brewery, rescued him. He started out life with one abusive family, and then another. Amazingly, after being adopted once more, this little guy became a therapy dog until his owner passed away. Maybe that's why, according to Sean, "Buddy has no manners." Buddy now happily follows Sean's daughter around, nibbling on the goodies she drops.

Rocco

Favorite Treat: Bacon

Annoying Habit: Chews bones on the bed in the middle of the night

Favorite Activity: Car rides with his head out the window

Buddy

Annoying Habit: Crying in the car

Mischievous Act: Sneaking out of the garage to hang out in the "hood"

Favorite Toy: Squeaky duck

Rocco, who became part of the family when Sean married his wife Erin, is definitely a BrewDog. When Sean started out brewing in the garage, Rocco decided this was his favorite place to hang out.

Rocco, Age 8, Cockapoo & Buddy, Age 7, Papillon   Owner: Sean Nook

Sedna

Sedna

Funny Habit: Bows her head when she wants to be petted forcing people to pet her

Naughtiest Deed: Unspooled all of the toilet paper

Best Trick: Rolls over and plays dead

Opened Summer 2012

Award winning Brewmaster: Julius Hummer

Louisville's first brewery

They could have a dog rodeo at the Chapman house. Grimm Brothers brewer and owner Don Chapman may be looking ahead thinking that his two little girls, Inara, age four, and Elsa, two, could compete. "They both are learning to ride on the backs of Sedna and on our other dog, Galileo. The dogs love it and the girls think it's fun." Don says. "They are getting to be pretty good little riders." When they get a little older, will the girls be getting horses? Living in Loveland, Colorado, that should be no problem.

Sedna came from a litter of farm puppies in Fort Collins and has been a loyal, ("crazy loyal," according to Don) member of the family. At age ten her favorite vantage point is the back deck, and her favorite pastime is hanging out with the guys.

Sedna, Age 10, St. Bernard / Border Collie Mix   Owner: Don Chapman

Harley

Founded May 2012

Century old location was originally "City Star Livery Stable"

Gold Medal, 2013 US Open Beer Championship," Bandit Brown", English Brown Ale

Harley

Favorite Toy: Doesn't play with toys, never got to be a puppy

Annoying Habit: Snores-deeper and louder than you would think

Most Excellent Adventure: Going on road trips to rescue other dogs

A power washer put out his eye when they were cleaning his cage. Fortunately Harley survived the harshness of the puppy mill to be rescued by National Mill Dog Rescue and adopted by Whitney and John Way, owners of City Star Brewing. Harley has become a Facebook sensation ("Harley Freight Train Ferguson") with nearly 30,000 "likes" spreading awareness of puppy mill abuse across the country. John and Whitney have participated in rescues. "It's amazing to see these dogs run for the first time," she comments. "He's bowlegged and has only one eye so he's developed a bit of a John Wayne swagger" says Whitney, "Harley is a real trooper." We even named a beer after him, Harley's "Ole' One Eye Honey Wheat."

IN DOG BEERS, I'VE ONLY HAD ONE

Harley, Age 12, Chihuahua   Owners: Whitney and John Way

Gomez

TELLURIDE BREWING COMPANY
TELLURIDE

Founded October 2011

Face Down Brown Ale 2012 double gold medals GABF and World Beer Cup

2013: Expanded distribution throughout Colorado

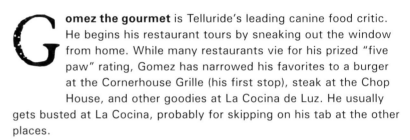

Gomez the gourmet is Telluride's leading canine food critic. He begins his restaurant tours by sneaking out the window from home. While many restaurants vie for his prized "five paw" rating, Gomez has narrowed his favorites to a burger at the Cornerhouse Grille (his first stop), steak at the Chop House, and other goodies at La Cocina de Luz. He usually gets busted at La Cocina, probably for skipping on his tab at the other places.

Tommy Thacher, Telluride Brewing Company's President, says Gomez started early as a foodie. At nine months of age while on a two night rafting trip, he slipped out of camp. Secretly he visited a campsite a couple of miles downstream and raided their food coolers. The next day Gomez was spotted by his victims who shouted, "there's the bear that raided our camp last night!" as they floated past his raft. Tommy had to row especially fast.

Gomez

First Meeting: At a truck stop in Fountain, Colorado

Favorite Food: Steak (surprise)

Naughtiest Deed: Ate a closet full of girl's underwear, costing Tommy a couple of paychecks

Gomez, Age 8, Basset Hound   Owner: Tommy Thacher

Samson

ELK MOUNTAIN BREWING
PARKER

Established 2009

2010 and 2011 Silver Medal Colorado State Fair for "Ghost Town Brown"

2012 Pilsner 3rd place All Colorado Beer Festival

Samson

Favorite Treat: Popcorn

Funny Habit: Always begs for treats before dinner

Gets Excited: A ride in the car

"**H**e ate a friend's binoculars on a camping trip,"** says Tom Bell, Brewer/Owner at Elk Mountain Brewery. Tom admits that Samson loves camping because of the smells, and evidently that day the binoculars smelled good. But then again, he doesn't have any toys because he eats them too! Samson was adopted from the Denver Dumb Friends League when he was one. He has a gentle and loving personality and helped Tom's wife and co-owner Marcia, overcome her fear of dogs. He doesn't bark which gives him the perfect demeanor to be the BrewDog at Elk Mountain. Samson was Tom's brewing companion when he was making gold medal winning beer for amateur competition. Now after going pro he is happy to see Tom continue to earn awards for his beers.

Samson, Age 11, Black Labrador   Owners: Tom and Marcia Bell

Rogue

Rogue

Naughtiest Deed: While a puppy, chewed up a bed frame that Brian had built

Favorite Treat: Real bones and when necessary, just a stick

Best Trick: Can balance a bone on her nose, flip it, and catch it

RENEGADE BREWING COMPANY
DENVER

Founded 2011

In Spring 2013 opened second location "Renegade Publik House" near University of Denver

Selected "best neighborhood brewery 2012" by Denver's Westword Newspaper

Thanks Dad, I can finally be a BrewDog!...Brewer/Owner Brian O'Connell adopted Rogue from a shelter ten years ago. Now in her retirement years she leads a BrewDog's life by hanging out at Renegade Brewing. Rogue warmly greets each customer at the door and has gotten to know the regulars. Like any good 'bark-keep', she's a good listener, and knows where all the dog bones are buried. Don't worry though,

Rogue is not a gossip. What she hears at the brewery, stays at the brewery! When Rogue isn't at Renegade, she enjoys hunting down the shady spots on her walks in the park, and capturing long naps.

Originally from upstate New York, Brian, Renegade's owner, attended University of Arizona, with grad work in Vermont and Florida. After these cross country moves Rogue is glad to be settling in Colorado.

Rogue, Age 10, Australian Shepherd   Owner: Brian O'Connell

Annie Hall

HALL BREWING COMPANY
PARKER

Annie Hall

Most Excellent Adventure: Airplane ride

Mischievous Act: Loves to antagonize the cat

Favorite Hobby: Sleeping

Opened January 2013

Brewery was built from Colorado beetle kill pine

Beers named "Farmhouse" because the brewery is on the family farm

She's a princess all right... after a long day of royal duties which includes standing on her back legs and waving to her subjects like the queen, Annie insists that her staff bring her Kraft cheese singles before they tuck her into her pink fluffy bed. Other royal activities include exercise, which consists of running laps around the dining table, and swimming. When she travels out of town for state visits she prefers the respectful opulence of the Fairmont Hotel.

Annie Hall, Age 3, Shih Tzu   Owners: Aubrey & Sue Hall

Radar

Founded in 2011 by former schoolteacher

2012 Colorado State Fair Gold Medal: "Outa Range Pale Ale"

2013 Added patio seating to current location

Radar

Favorite Hangout: The brewery

Most Excellent Adventure: While camping nearly got lost in the tall grass

Funny Habit: Doesn't like 'people' food, so he leaves the room at meal times.

"**H**e got his name because of his oversized ears"... says Lone Tree sales and events manager, Bridgette Geiger. A true BrewDog, Radar has been around the brewery since it started. He likes to hang out at the bar and be part of the scene.

His 'radar' was working one day, when a new customer came in and sat at the bar. Radar was sitting in 'his' chair, but suddenly got up and climbed into the customer's lap. When the bartender apologized, the customer said, "Oh no, that's ok, I had to put my dog down this morning." Radar stayed with him for about an hour. The customer is now a regular, and Radar got a raise.

Radar, Age 3, Rat Terrier / Chihuahua Owner: Bridgette Geiger

Maceo

Asher Brewing Co.
Boulder, Colorado

Maceo

Best Trick: Balancing a pint of beer on his head

Excellent Adventure: Walked several miles home from the brewery looking for Chris

Funny Habit: Very good at catching flies

Established November 2009

Colorado's first organic brewery

Brewer Chris Asher won three GABF medals before starting Asher Brewing Co.

" **I think he's a reincarnated monk, he's so mellow and calm,"** says Chris Asher, owner of Asher Brewing. For example, he doesn't play with his toys, he just cuddles with them. Maceo is one of eleven puppies in his litter. They were all adopted through Golden Retriever Freedom Rescue of Denver. Chris says that once he attended a "family reunion" and nine of eleven puppies attended!

Maceo is at the brewery three days a week. His job is public relations, and quality control for customers buying food from the trucks that sell at the brewery. That means sampling, of course!

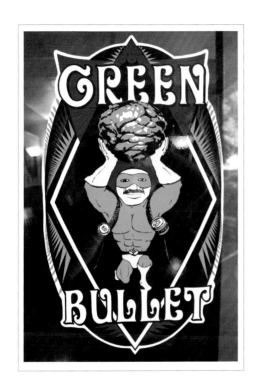

Maceo, Age 7, Golden Retriever Mix   Owner, Chris Asher

Burton & Betty

DRY DOCK BREWING COMPANY
AURORA

Founded 2005

Award winning beers. . .14 GABF medals since 2008 including 3 Gold

2013 Completed new production facility to allow statewide distribution

A Bulldog Cinderella story. . . Burton, second generation descendant of the legendary, and highly decorated three time Westminster champion English Bulldog stud Ch. Cherokee Legend Rock, meets beautiful Betty, the rescue dog from the Denver Dumb Friends League. They have Dry Dock's operations director Doug Hyndman to thank for their "fairy tail" romance.

Betty's favorite toys are Burtons, and Burton's are Betty's. Their favorite game is tug of war. . .with each other. They really are best friends. While Betty and Burton like to take walks with Doug, a mile almost overwhelmed Burton, who needed to be revived with a water hose afterwards.

Burton

Favorite Toy: Whatever Betty is playing with

Naughtiest Deed: Ate twenty DVDs when he was a puppy

Favorite Pastime: Napping

Betty

Favorite Toy: Whatever Burton is playing with

Naughtiest Deed: Throwing her bed around the house... bulldog "feng shui"

Favorite Hangout: Beanbag in the sunroom

Maß (pr. Moss)

Second largest craft beer producer in Colorado

Opened second brewery in Brevard, North Carolina in 2012

2011 three medals at GABF, two silver and one bronze

"**He was the roly-poly chubby one**. I adopted him from a litter born while being fostered by a family volunteering with Aussie Dog Rescue of Colorado," explained Lauren Wiersma, who is among a small but growing group of female brewers in Colorado. She had become involved as a volunteer with the Aussie Dog rescue group, and had provided foster shelter to several dogs before adopting Maß.

In a short time he has managed to make an impression. He was the culprit who showed the other two dogs in the house how to get through the garden fence, and was an accomplice to eating all of the vegetables. He can also break into the laundry room.

He likes to crouch down in the yard to pounce on the other dogs, but he's still a clumsy puppy and always misses.

Maß

Favorite Pastime: Belly scratches

Most Excellent Adventure: Brewery tour right after he was adopted

Naughtiest Deed: Steals beer cans from the recycle bin; Dales Pale Ale cans are his first choice

Maß (pr. Moss), Age 4 months, Australian Shepherd/ Cattle Dog Mix
Owners: Lauren Wiersma and Logan Wiley

Mosely

Founded early 2013

One of ten favorite nano-breweries by "Bon Appetite Magazine"

Company slogan, "Beer for All"

"**He purrs when you pet him,**" says Angie Grenz, who with husband Josh, are partners in Verboten Brewing. "Angie and I both love Basset Hounds. Mosely is our second. Several years ago we had to give up Herman our first basset, because we moved. Our best friends adopted him and when we moved back, Mosely and Herman became good friends." adds Josh.

Mosely likes to strut his stuff at the dog park. "He likes to play rough

with the big dogs. He's short but pretty stout, so he holds his own," says Josh. "What's really fun is to watch him play in the snow. He's too short to run in it, so he jumps like a rabbit."

Mosely

Naughtiest Deed: Stole a whole chicken from the table and ate it!

Favorite Toy: "Big Mouth"-A toy filled with tennis balls that the dog works to remove

Funny Habit: Howls and barks at fire trucks

Mosely, Age 4, Basset Hound   Owners: Josh and Angie Grenz

Hyde

Founded October 2012

"Roots" of the company are in Windsor Gardens, a greenhouse grower

Father and son family business

Mr. Hyde

Favorite Toy: Rubber eggplant, has had since a puppy

Naughtiest Deed: Broke into chicken coop and ate the eggs

Annoying Habit: Panting hot air onto your face

Better behave, Mr. Hyde is watching and he sees everything from the platform in the Brewhouse. "He's a BrewDog all right," says Zach Weakland, brewer and co-owner of High Hops Brewing, "He just loves to be up there." Zach continues, "When he's not in the Brewhouse, we have the perfect place for a high energy farm dog, since we also have a family greenhouse plus a hop farm." One day, when he was two, Hyde wasn't paying attention and was hit by a car. "That was a scary time." says Zach. "He had surgery and survived, but he lost half of a lung." Hyde has decided that the Brewhouse is safer than the street.

Hyde, Age 4, Border Collie / Australian Shepherd   Owner: Zach Weakland

Hubert

Established December 2011

Bronze Medal, Colorado State Fair: Helles

Canning beer in 2014

Hubert

Best Trick: Does a front handstand when he eats

Best Adventure: Bodysurfing in Hawaii in his own life jacket

Second Best Trick: Can walk on his front legs

His front legs are like "Schwarzenegger's"...Hubert was born with a disability causing his back legs to be permanently hyper extended. "He has adapted by developing his front legs to compensate" says Josh West, Lone Tree's assistant brewer. Josh's wife worked at the humane society in Hawaii where they rescued Hubert just before he was to be euthanized. He weighed less than a pound then, but has bulked up to around eight pounds.

He can't jump up on the couch or run up the stairs like other dogs," says Josh, "but he makes up for that with lots of love."

Hubert, Age 3, Rat Terrier / Chihuahua Owner: Josh West

Pearl

BRISTOL BREWING COMPANY
COLORADO SPRINGS

Cheyenne Canon Pinon Nut Ale, Bronze Medal 2011 GABF

Tuesdays host Karma Hour with a donation for every pint to designated charity

February 2013, opened Bristol Taproom at Colorado Springs Airport

She looked like a little pearl, she was so white as a puppy. She may come from a line of AKC Champions, but that doesn't make a difference to the cat. "The cat is the boss," says Tom Zurenko, Bristol's General Manager. "The cat takes the bed and Pearl sleeps on the floor." Kelty, a thirteen year old rescue cat, has mentored Pearl in a lot of ways. She taught her to groom herself like a cat, and Pearl even purrs like her feline friend!

Pearl knows that her role in the home is to give love and affection. In return she loves to be petted, and will give you lots of nuzzles to persuade you to keep going. When Tom is out of town she sneaks into bed with his wife, Suzan. When he is at home she never leaves his side. Find Tom and you will find Pearl.

Pearl

Naughtiest Deeds: Shredded a lot of dog beds

Favorite Food: Broccoli

Best Friend/Accomplice: Kelty the Cat

Pearl, Age 7, Golden Retriever Owner: Tom Zurenko

Lucy

Lucy

Funny Habit: Growls for attention

Not Favorite Pastime: Walks-- hides when she sees the leash

Annoying Habit: Snatches food from the kids, Abby (12) and Bailey (9)

Founded 1994, Under current ownership since 2003

Renegade IPA award GABF (Gold, 1993) and Word Beer Championship (Silver, 2003)

Started bottling in 1995

She gets grumpy on cloudy days, it's a good thing she lives in Colorado. She loves to sun herself and finds the sunny spots in the house throughout the day.

Brewery owners Tyler and Kim Lemirande say that when she was a puppy she was mentored by their cat Mittens, who developed her "catlike" agility. She jumps from the back of the sofa to the chair and then to the recliner, and finally onto the breakfast table looking for a meal.

Sometimes she escapes from the yard and is impossible to catch. "We call her Lightning Loosey Goosey Lucy, because she is so quick," says Kim, "we have to lure her back with food."

Lucy, Age 2, English Bulldog   Owners: Tyler and Kim Lemirande

OMG!
(don't look)

there are. . . **CATS** in this book

that's ok there are some cool cats inviting you to some cold beer

Frank the Tank

Established 2011

2012 Gold Medal GABF, Mexican Chocolate Stout

2012 Westword Magazine best brewery for neighbors

A cat who thinks he's a dog? According to brewery owners Kristen and Jeremy, Frank, who was rescued from the pound eight years ago came with some very "un-cat" like traits. He wears a harness and likes to go for walks on a leash (he loves the leash), he raids the trash can (they had to Velcro the lid shut), and he comes when he is called (how many cats come when they are called?).

Frank's job at the brewery is master fly catcher and when he is off duty he hangs out in the tasting room with the regulars. In fact, Frank is so popular they named their new fermenter after him, and Frank got a nick name, "Frank the Tank."

"Frank the Tank"

Most Excellent Adventure: Riding on the dashboard during a road trip from North Carolina

Best Trick: Sits still for treats (is he really a cat?)

Favorite Toy: A stuffed mouse, of course!

Frank the Tank, Age 8, Tuxedo Cat Owners: Kristen Kozik and Jeremy Gobien

Ash

Cool Cats... Cold Beer

Ash the C-Monster, Age 3 Tuxedo

The Alpha regulator, bosses all the other cats: Top Cat,

Relentless regulation just beats up the other cats

Main competitor for John's affection

He's my boy, he's my son, we've been though a lot together and I know I will be saying goodbye soon," said John Schneider, head brewer," as he choked back some tears. Bailey, aka "The Shark," is John's first and oldest cat. He and wife Nichole both share the same emotional bond with their cats, as others feel towards their dogs. This clowder (group of cats) has its own social structure in the Schneider house. Ash "The

C-Monster" rules as the alpha male and regulates the others. He keeps the older cats in place (Bailey and Marilyn) while he competes for John and Nichole's attention and affection. Tinker is his "Gangsta Mama" plaything. Berg is the loner in the group.

Berg, Age 14, Ragamuffin

A loner, isolated by the other cats

"Rescued from a dangerous family situation"

Poses, and likes to look pretty

Climbs trees but can't get down

Marilyn, Tinker & Bailey

Cool Cats... Cold Beer

Dry Dock, Cat Dynamics

Ash, CMonster

Alpha Male
"The Regulator"

Tinker

Ash's plaything
"Gangsta Mama"

Bailey

"The Shark"
Living out his last days

Berg

Social Outcast
"The Loner"

Marilyn

Bailey's nemesis, now
peaceful coexistence

Marilyn, Age 15, Sylvester / Tuxedo

Adopted at Pet Smart to be a companion for Bailey

Had been abused, hides when John takes off his belt

Bailey and Marilyn hated each other...cat fights

Now they are both old, they tolerate each other

Tinker, Age 2 1/2, Calico

As kitten, rescued from a creek bed
abandoned, starving and sick

Is Ash's (C-Monster) play mate, even if he
hurts her

She is his "Gangsta Mama"

Bailey, Age 15, Tortoise Shell Tabby

"Dreampower" adoption

John and Nichole's first cat

Old and in his last days

Deacon & Sage

GABF Medals for TPS Report (American Wild Ale): Gold 2009, Bronze 2012

Pub features "slow food" with locally sourced organic products

2012 Expansion increased capacity by 300%

"**They're a couple of Frisbee sluts,**" says Tom Brown, Trinity's lead brewer. Deacon will do back flips and jump six feet in the air to catch a Frisbee. Sage loves Frisbees, but will retrieve anything you toss her way, just for the sport of it. If they don't have squirrels or balls to run after, they will chase each other.

"Mischief is in their DNA," says Tom. Sage found a bottle Bailey's on the counter, figured out a way to open it and drank the whole thing! Deacon once innocently got into a chicken coup to "play" thinking that the young chickens were toys. It was a tough day for the chickens.

Deacon

Most Excellent Adventure: Disappeared for two days, then returned home as if nothing had happened

Annoying Habit: Whines when he needs attention

Personality: 'Hyper-energetic'

Sage

Best Trick: Balancing Bacon on her nose

Most Excellent Adventure: Working with Tom as a fishing guide in Alaska

Favorite Hangout: Bear Creek Dog Park

Sage, Age 11, Australian Shepherd & Deacon, Age 6, Australian Shepherd   Owner: Tom Brown   61

Billie

Billie

Favorite Toy: Blue Dragon, her first toy and it's still intact

Annoying Habit: Moves clothes around the house

Excellent Adventure: Road trip to Florida, played in the ocean

Started Canning 2013

Brewery and tasting room 100% powered by wind energy

February 2010 received organic certification for all beers

"**When the bike stops, she doesn't,**" says Jules Masters, Asher's office manager. "She's still learning how to run alongside my bike. "Since her adoption from Boulder County Humane Society as a three month old puppy, Billie has been learning quickly, but still has more to do. She knows more than she is letting on though, and plays a game with Jules. When she's off leash with Jules she won't come back. If Jules runs towards her she runs away, so to catch her, Jules runs away. Billie will chase and Jules lets herself "get caught." Aha, Billie gets back on the leash.

"She is super enthusiastic about life" says Jules, "and loves to be anywhere people are. She doesn't want to miss a thing."

Billie, Age 1, Lab / Whippet   Owner: Jules Masters

Doobie

Founded January 2010

Eagle County's only production brewery

Vail Valley Chamber of Commerce 2013 Mid-Size Business of the Year

What does a 100 pound Chocolate Lab become at Halloween? A bear of course! Doobie and his 120 lb father escaped from the brewery to prowl the Eagle River walkway, and the whole community was abuzz about the "bears" on the Riverwalk!

To remove other insinuations, we must clarify that Doobie is named for brewer/owner Kevin's favorite childhood stuffed animal "PaDuBaBub, which is a mouthful hence, "Doobie."

Doobie is "tennis ball obsessed," so Kevin and Marisa acquired a basket of practice balls from the tennis club and surprised Doobie with a roomful of his favorite toys! He went crazy as he tried to chase down each bouncy treasure.

Doobie

Favorite Hangout: The Crazy Mountain tasting room-a true BrewDog

Naughtiest Deed: Broke open a full keg of beer at home ruining the hardwood floors

Funny Habit: Buries his head under pillows and thinks he is hiding!

Doobie, Age 4, English Labrador Retriever   Owners: Kevin and Marisa Selvy

Starfox & Crixus

Opened 2010 in Northeast Denver

Award winning flagship beer Lao Wang, a spiced Asian Lager

Second location in Lakewood, Co. 2013

From cyberspace to ancient Rome. Starfox, named for the video game, thought he was a one of its warriors when he attempted to "fly" down brewery owners Danny and Betty's stairs. The "flight" ended with a broken leg, which required a metal splint. He is now a "bionic dog."

Crixus' namesake led a rebellion against Caesar, but perhaps should be more aptly named "Circus." Shortly after her adoption from the Dumb Friends League, her groomer decided to dye her tail! The bright blue tail and tutu got plenty of attention, which she loved.

Starfox

Favorite Toy: His girlfriend, a stuffed cat; he gets a new one every year

Best Trick: He's a really good dancer with his "bionic" leg

Best Friend: Crixus

Crixus

Favorite Toy: A purple rope

Funny Habit: Wedges between cushions to sleep

Best Friend: Starfox

Crixus, Age 3, Pomeranian & Starfox, Age 4, Pomeranian   Owners: Danny and Betty Wang

Cahoots (Hoots)

Committed to quality, hand crafted, innovative beers

2007 GABF Gold Medal for Odell IPA

Charity is important at Odell and an employee committee manages giving

"**Big dogs, little dogs, red dogs, blue dogs...What a dog party!**" Hoots invited all the neighborhood dogs just like a page out of the old children's book, *Go, Dog, Go!* What favors did he give at his second birthday party? Bones, of course!

Cats, well he plays with them differently. He gives them a little nibble and puts their heads in his mouth, but doesn't bite them. Josh Leeman, Odell's wholesale manager, doesn't know how he gets them to cooperate. Maybe Hoots invited them to his party or pays them off in tuna. "He is the best dog, almost perfect, he's only peed in the house once!"

Hoots

Funny Habit: He sleeps on his back with his paws behind his head

Most Excellent Adventure: Met a porcupine on a backpacking trip. . . Ouch!

Gets Excited By: Falling snow, it's party time

Cahoots (Hoots), Age 2, Bernese Mt. Dog / Huskie Mix   Owner: Josh Leeman

Otis

Opened March 2008

Silver Medal GABF 2012 for "French Belgian Saison"

Second floor tasting room has view of Aspen Mountain

Otis

Favorite pastime: Napping in the grain room at the brewery ("malt head")

Best trick: Jumps up and gives a "high five"

Favorite treat: Bar pretzels

"**O**tis My Man" is the nickname of the coolest doggie dude in Aspen, Colorado. If you have ever been to Aspen, that's saying something. Muscular, and masculine, Otis is a "chick magnet" and can be seen hanging with Aspen's coolest babes, both canine and human, although Emma, a black lab, is his number one girl.

According to Aspen Brewing Company's founder Duncan Claus, Otis is an excellent athlete. He skis with him (most recently "skied/body surfed" down Walsh's run), has plans to summit a fourteener, and is an avid trail runner. His favorite run is the seventeen miles to and from Conundrum Hot Springs, which was the inspiration for Aspen Brewing's "Conundrum Red" ale. Ladies, get in line!

Otis, Age 4, American Pit Bull Terrier Owner: Duncan Claus

Suzu

VERY NICE BREWING COMPANY
NEDERLAND

Founded 2012

Friendly, warm atmosphere

Special brews with portion of sales to local charities

Suzu

Favorite Treat: Treats are new, just learning

Best Trick: Chases tail when she gets excited

Favorite Pastime: Going in and out of the doggie door; a new discovery

"**S**he's 11 and finally learning to be a dog,** after spending her whole life in a cage, as a breeding dog in a puppy mill," says brewery co-owner, Susan. Three weeks ago Susan and husband Jeff gave Suzu a 'forever home' through Sheba Scout Rescue. Susan continued, "Everything is new, like going for walks, being around people and other dogs. Still very timid, she's an old lady just getting used to things."

Having another dog (Phil) in the house has been a big help. "He makes her feel safe and he has been helping her explore new surroundings," said Susan with a smile. "He's teaching her the value of begging, so she is spending more time with us in the kitchen."

Suzu, Age 11, Shiba Inu   Owners: Jeff and Susan Green

Vera

Vera

Funny /Habit: Runs in circles

Best Friend/Accomplice: Honey

Favorite Hangout: Living room couch

LOVELAND ALEWORKS
LOVELAND

Owner/ Brewer Nick Callaway studied Physics and Engineering

Went "pro" in 2012 after years of home brewing

Located in historic downtown Loveland

Vera was a ballplayer in her earlier life, or at least that's how is seems. She can catch the deep fly ball as well as the high heat. That's pretty good for a dog. "She and our other dog, Honey are quite a pair," says brewery owner Nick Callaway.

Since the baby came, Honey snuggles with her but Vera sees her as a food source." Evidently, Vera likes to sneak up and steal the baby's graham crackers. Her scavenging has a positive side though, because she picks up the food under the high chair.

Years ago in a "sibling brawl" between the two dogs, Vera broke Honey's tail. "They have been best friends ever since," says Nick.

Vera, Age 7, German Shepherd Mix & Honey, Age 10, Chow Mix
Owners: Nick Callaway and Kari Klapper

Pearl

Founded 1989 in a converted grain elevator

Colorado's second and Fort Collins' first craft brewery

2012 Founders Corkie Odell and brother Doug and his wife Wynne, Received the prestigious Brewers Association Special Recognition Award.

Pearl

Favorite Toy: Stuffed Squirrel

Best Trick: "Sits real nice" but also can do " high five"

Annoying Habit: Gets jealous when Corkie and her husband hug each other

"Queen of the house"...is how Pearl acts when she gets all dressed up in her very own Poodle skirt. Corkie Odell's grandkids think Pearl is a real hoot, almost like having a crazy aunt! "She's sweet and really is a good girl", says the brewery co-founder. One of Pearl's favorite pastimes is napping on Corkie's pontoon boat on "the lake". One afternoon she got a big surprise though. She fell in and discovered she didn't know how to swim. Whoops! Maybe Pearl should stick to her favorite dry land activity; walking around the lake with Corkie.

Pearl, Age 5, Standard Poodle Owner: Corkie Odell

Rocky

Rocky

Best Friend: Camilla the dog

Girlfriend: Molly-Camilla is Jealous

Favorite Hangout: Camilla's house

Opened Summer 2012

Award winning Brewmaster: Julius Hummer

Louisville's first brewery

He ran through the screen door to catch the skunk. "The house stunk to high heaven for days," said John Frazee, one of Gravity's co-founders and brewers. Rocky is a big, intimidating dog whose deep mastiff bark strikes fear in the hearts of John's visitors. When John says "It's your friend," he stops barking and cries with excitement. Actually, John thought he had adopted an eight week old Australian Shepherd from the Boulder Humane Society, so you can imagine his surprise when Rocky kept getting bigger and bigger. Even the experts can be fooled. Being a big dog inspired John and his partners to name a beer after him: "Hound Beast," a big barley wine that comes in at 13% ABV.

Rocky, Age 7, Mastiff/Labrador Mix   Owner: John Frazee

Daisy

HALL BREWING COMPANY
PARKER

Wood for brewery was milled by hand from beetle kill pine logs

Tasting room is in Town of Parker

Hand crafted beers from a hand crafted brewery

Daisy

Favorite Pastime: Wrestling with Otis

Gets Excited: Rabbits

Favorite Hangout: In the lab at the brewery

Keep her away from the laundry, or you will find it scattered around. "She has her own method of sorting clothes" says Hall Brewing owner Aubrey Hall, "so if my socks don't match, you will know why." Daisy and her partner Otis, also an Aussie Shepherd mix, joined the Hall household at the same time. That's a lot of herd dog puppy energy at once. "I thought it was a good idea at the time," says Aubrey, "What was I thinking?" Fortunately Daisy and Otis have a farm to run on and can hang out in the Hall farmhouse brewery.

Daisy, Age 6 months, Australian Sheep Dog/ Border Collie Mix   Owner: Aubrey Hall

EO

Beers inspired by both American and European craft beer traditions

Wide variety of seasonal offerings

July 3, 2013 Fest of Ale-- First Anniversary Celebration

EO

Favorite Pastime: Trying to herd the cat

Annoying Habit: Won't sleep anywhere but on the bed, preferably on Casey's pillow

Excellent Adventure: Camping in Oregon's Crater Lake National Park

H**e was a dog with no name,** actually he had a name but no one knew what it was. "He was given to me by some friends, who rescued him from a shelter in Cheyenne, Wyoming." Casey Funderburk, tap room manager shared. "I had always wanted a dog and when I saw him I fell in love," she confided. The shelter in Cheyenne named him Sam, but "he didn't respond," says Casey, "so I tried dozens of names with no luck. Finally, I tried EO, after Edward Osborn Wilson, the biologist, and I got his attention." She learned later that lots of border collies are called Oreo because of their coloration, so she concluded that his original name was probably Oreo.

EO, Age 10, Border Collie Mix   Owner: Casey Funderburk

Maya

Greenhouse and Brewery are together

Hop farm on property, grow 54 varieties

People's choice Gnarly Barley Beer Festival 2013

Maya

Best Friend: Zach

Naughtiest Deed: Was left in car and bit a chunk out of Zach's steering wheel

Favorite Treat: Pre-fermented beer because it's sweet

Save the pizza crust for Maya, since that's her favorite treat. That probably means that Zach Wheatland, co-owner and brewer, and his family eat a lot of pizza. Somewhere there's a story about Maya eating a whole pizza, but she's not talking. Maya mostly hangs out at Windsor Gardens which is a three generation family business, and co-located with the High Hops Brewery. She is the unofficial greeter, "and 'gooses' everyone, as she welcomes them" says Zach. They must have very easy going customers, are good at apologies, or have great beer.

Maya, Age 6, Labrador / German Shepherd Mix   Owner: Zach Weakland

Moby & Annie

Established 2013

First brewery in Englewood Colorado

The nation's only brewery that "brews" both coffee and beer

When they saw the fresh kill, they knew it was a lion . . . brewer/owner Paul and his family were grateful that Moby and Annie had chased the cat away. When the Webster's forage for mushrooms in Colorado's back country they take Moby, the "gentle giant" Leonberger / Bernese mix at eighty-eight pounds and Annie, the eighty-four pound great Pyrenees/Afghan mix . These two enthusiastically patrol the forest together. According to Suzanne, "Annie is developing a good nose for mushrooms, she may even become a truffle dog."

Rescued from a Philadelphia shelter, the twelve week old, forty-two pound "little Moby" came on a flight that included an eight and a half hour delay! The flight attendants made sure he had first class treatment though by paying him frequent visits as he waited. Upon arrival his new owners rushed to the baggage claim to greet him.

Moby

Best Trick: The "Leo-Paw". He puts his (big) paw on you to get your attention; a Leonberger trait

Naughtiest Deed: "Counter surfing". He is tall enough to steal anything from the kitchen counter, including prime filet **mignon!**

Funny Habit: Pulls the covers off the bed to wake you up

Annie

Naughtiest Deed: Swimming in backyard pond and then lounging on the sofa

Favorite Hangout: The brewery "The Bob." She was there every day during construction

Annoying Habit: Jumping up to say "hello"

Moby, Age 6, Leonberger/Bernese & Annie, Age 2, Great Pyrenees/Afghan Hound
Owners: Paul and Suzanne Webster

Louis

Louis

Favorite Toy: Rubber lizard

Funny Habit: Likes to lie on top of his pal Gomez, the Basset Hound

Favorite Pastime: Hiking and running trails around Telluride

Tasting room has no chairs because of Telluride City regulations

First beers in cans: Angel Veil Pale Ale, and award winning Face Down Brown

Fish Water Double IPA is named after co-owner and head brewer Chris Fish

Mellow and Energetic seem polar opposites, to describe Louis (pronounced, Loo-eee). At four months, this puppy's best trick is being cute! He hangs out with Telluride Brewing Company's other BrewDog, Gomez, who is teaching him a thing or two. Already Louis's favorite food is steak.

Louis is a second-generation family dog says his owner Wynne Calcutt, fiancé of Tommy Thacher, President of Telluride Brewing Company. "I grew up with Jack Russell Terriers, so when my parents said they had a litter of pups, we chose Louis."

Little Louis once escaped from a soft crate on an airplane trip, while Wynne was sleeping. She was awakened by screams from twenty rows up as Louis ran up the aisle and under seats. Don't tell Homeland Security about that one.

Louis, Age 4 months, Jack Russell Terrier   Owner: Wynne Calcutt

Cletus Hercules

"Eco-sensitivity" is a major corporate theme

Pub interior built almost entirely with recycled materials

Recycle all glass, plastic and metal waste they produce

Cletus Hercules

Best Trick: He pulls other dogs around by their collars

Funny Quirk: Fear of the veterinarian's scale extends to other rectangles like pizza boxes

Mischievous Act: Scatters the cat litter

H**e likes books and Barbie dolls.** He chews up the books, but he hides the Barbie dolls. "It's going to be interesting when I find where he's stashed them," said Johannah Murphy, tasting room manager. "He's a giant dog who still thinks he's a puppy, so he is very playful." He is rough and tumble with other dogs, and really gentle with babies. He lets them crawl all over him. After all that activity it's time for a peanut butter and bacon cong and nap time.

When he was adopted from the humane society at eight weeks old he was fourteen pounds and his paws "were as big as my hand" says Johannah. Now he has grown into his paws but as Johannah says, he is still "sweet and goofy."

Cletus Hercules, Age 1 1/2, Mastiff / Rhodesian Ridgeback Owner: Johannah Murphy

Otis

Otis

Favorite Toy: Tennis balls -- surprise!

Excellent Adventure: Driving the fork lift, co-pilot of course

Best Trick: Still learning how to "shake"

Brewer owner Aubrey Hall learned to brew from Grandfather

Most of Brewery built by hand

Hops are grown on the farm

He digs up the flowers, and co-owner Sue Hall just plants them again. After all that digging he goes next door and plays in the waterfall in the neighbor's backyard. Although he is still just a puppy, brewer Aubrey Hall says that Otis is learning to be a BrewDog. He hangs out with his accomplice Daisy (also a six month old Aussie Shepherd mix), at their farmhouse brewery just East of Parker. He hasn't realized yet that the beers are not for puppies. "I really have to watch him," says Aubrey. At the end of the day, Otis arranges his bed and lies on his back happily dreaming about his next day as a BrewDog.

Otis, Age 6 months, Australian Shepherd/ Heeler   Owners: Aubrey Hall and Sue Hall

Cash

Founded in 2010 (after closure of a previous brewery)

Dirty Hippy Dark Wheat beer is best seller

Perennial "People's Choice" winner at beer events

Cash

Annoying Habit: Chasing chickens, Danny now has to buy his eggs.

Favorite Toy: Rocks! Throw them and he will retrieve all day long

Favorite Hangout: Fishing camp on the river with Danny

At the brewery from the beginning, Cash is the main BrewDog who runs the show at the Palisade Brewing Company. If visiting dogs get too rowdy, he keeps them in line with the bark of an order. Head brewer Danny Wilson adopted him from the local animal shelter when Cash was eight months old. "He was a lover from the start, but is also full of mischief. He likes to move stuff around," Cash's owner explained. Once he chewed through a heavy antique wooden door to rearrange Danny's garden seeds into piles. There was some explaining to do about the door to his landlady.

Cash, Age 4, Basenji German Shepherd Mix   Owner: Danny Wilson

Grizzly & Greta

Founded 2010

Specializing in "wild" sour beers, and saisons

2013 new brewery triples production, features rare Belgian "coolship" open air fermentation and cooling vessel

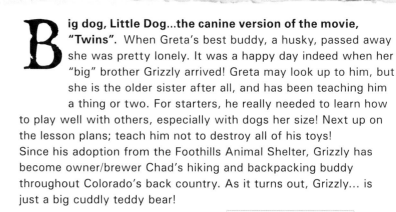

Big dog, Little Dog...the canine version of the movie, **"Twins".** When Greta's best buddy, a husky, passed away she was pretty lonely. It was a happy day indeed when her "big" brother Grizzly arrived! Greta may look up to him, but she is the older sister after all, and has been teaching him a thing or two. For starters, he really needed to learn how to play well with others, especially with dogs her size! Next up on the lesson plans; teach him not to destroy all of his toys!

Since his adoption from the Foothills Animal Shelter, Grizzly has become owner/brewer Chad's hiking and backpacking buddy throughout Colorado's back country. As it turns out, Grizzly... is just a big cuddly teddy bear!

Grizzly

Favorite Food: Raspberries!

Naughtiest Deed: Chews up fences

Annoying Habit: Destroys all his toys

Greta

Favorite Food: Carrots and Hash

Naughtiest Deed: Ran away for several days- returned dirty, and so fat from eating food from trash cans that her tummy dragged on the ground

Annoying Habit: Barks a lot!

Grizzly, Age 1, Siberian Husky & Greta, Age 7, Beagle   Owner: Chad and Silvana Yakobson   97

Cindy Loo

ODELL BREWING COMPANY
FORT COLLINS

Sustainable alternative energy supplies about 25% of overall demand

IPA Gold Medal, GABF 2007

Flagship beer is 90 Shilling Scottish Ale introduced in 1989

Cindy Loo

Mischievous Act: Steals avocados, eats them on the carpet, doesn't clean up

Annoying Habit: Pre-alarm morning wakeup call, with a paw to Matt's face

Naughtiest Deed: Ate a bag of sunflower seeds...they didn't digest, ('nough said)

Another white boxer, adopted...and Cindy Loo will be forever grateful to her new owner Matt Jaspers, who is Odell's tasting room manager. It is not unusual for white boxers to be born, but few survive. They have a genetic trait that causes them to be deaf and blind, so breeders euthanize the puppies. Fortunately these animals are now being rescued, and make terrific pets. Matt definitely agrees!

Still a puppy, Cindy Loo is discovering life, and the adventures it holds. How about the camping trip when she was attacked by flies...Calamine Lotion anyone? Or the time she got into trouble for using all the electrical cords in Matt's house as chew toys. . . It all melts away with her big smile and puppy snuggles.

Cindy Loo, Age 1, Boxer   Owner: Matt Jaspers

Pancho Villa

Colorado's first Microbrewery, established 1979

Two home brewer CU professors started the company in a goat shed on a Boulder area farm.

Solar panels heat all water in the Pub, kitchen, restrooms and sinks

Pancho Villa

Best Friend: Jeff "El Jefe"

Favorite Toy: Socks, hides them, runs with them, chews them

Gets Excited: Girl dogs

Hey lady, will you marry me? Like the revolutionary Pancho Villa whose pick up line was a proposal, this little guy thinks he's a Latin Lover. Most dogs perk up when they hear "squirrel" or "treats", not Pancho. Say a girl's name, like "Angel", or "Lucy" and he is at attention. When he was adopted from the Denver Dumb Friends League he only weighed three pounds. Jeff, "El Jefe" (The Boss) at Boulder Beer says, "Maybe that's why he is food obsessed. He will eat anything, even veggies!" He also warns "don't leave food in your pockets because he will chew a hole to get it." Pancho is now a healthy twelve pounds.

Pancho Villa, Age 3, Chihuahua Owners: Jeff and Michelle Brown

Tiger

TRINITY BREWING COMPANY
COLORADO SPRINGS

Founded 2008

Focus on "Saison" style beers

Christmas Eve tradition is tapping of the "Cherry Awaken Stout"

"**Tiger is really a gentle dog,**" says Kirk, Trinity's "Beer Purveyor and Beer Philanthropist."

His breed gets a bad rap because of the irresponsible behavior of many breeders and owners. "On the trail Kirk gets a little frustrated when he hears other hikers call out warnings of "pit bull, pit ahead. "He thinks that maybe he should warn Tiger about "people ahead."

Tiger is an affectionate and devoted companion. He sneaks into Kirk's bed without waking him. Kirk stayed awake one night to see how Tiger did it. "He slowly climbs up, one paw at a time, and leaves one leg dangling. Amazing, because he is not a small dog."

Tiger

First Meeting: Last puppy at the dog rescue

Favorite Hangout: Wherever Kirk is

Favorite Food: Bread helped him regain weight after serious illness

Tiger, Age 8, American Bull Terrier / Boxer Mix   Owner: Kurt Schipke

Mojo

Established 2010

Delivers kegs to local customers with a custom built tricycle

Chosen for Denver Post's 2013 Colorado top 10 Patios and Beer Gardens

Mojo

Best Friend: Barley the cat

Favorite Hangout: The office at the brewery, where he does "pawperwork"

Favorite Pastime: Biting at sprinklers

He can do a back flip to catch a Frisbee...People ask if Mojo competes in disk dog events. Equinox owner Shannon Westcott, says she is thinking about it because he is so eager and such an athlete. Mojo's athleticism comes from his breeding as a cattle dog, although since he moved to town he applies his herding skills to children and chickens. Leave it to Mojo, the children will not wander off and the chickens will definitely come home to roost.

His best friend, Barley the cat, keeps him entertained. He swats at the air in front of Mojo, who bites at the imaginary foe then sneezes. They repeat this game over and over again!

Mojo, Age 2, Australian Shepherd/Border Collie Owner: Shannon & Colin Westcott

Brie & Olie

Started in 2005 in the back of John Bricker's insurance office in Del Norte, CO

Family owned and operated

Chosen 2013 Brewer of the Year by Colorado Malting Company

Total domination by twenty five pounds of dog...(that's two dogs)! Beware THE STARE. This is Olie's secret to human mind reading, and mind control. Brie's force is her big dog, big boss attitude. These two mighty Italian Greyhounds have taken over at Three Barrel co-owner Will and Bridget's house...in a good way!

Several years ago Olie knew when Bridget had a serious illness, and intuitively became her therapy dog. He would lie on her tummy for hours every day, and comforted her through her tears. "He helped me get well," says Bridget.

Brie was adopted through the Italian Greyhound Rescue, Colorado, who rescued her from an abusive owner. Although she only weighs twelve pounds, she intimidates much larger dogs with her "trash talking" snarls and barks.

According to Bridget, Olie gets a new black spot for every naughty deed and he "gets new ones all the time."

Brie

Favorite Food: Green Beans

Annoying Habit: Snatching food from little kids

Favorite Hangout: In a sunny spot

Olie

Favorite Hangout: Under a blanket

Best Trick: Mind control

Favorite Hobby: Hide and seek. He hides toys and then uses mental telepathy to help you find them

Olie, Age 8 & Brie, Age 7, Italian Greyhounds Owners: Will and Bridget Kreutzer

Phil the Dog

"Fear no beer" attitude

Innovation is part of company mission

Embrace experimentation with ancient beer styles

Phil the Dog

Gets Excited: w-a-l-k, yes he can spell

Favorite Treat: Pigs ears

Best Trick: Throws his bowl when he is hungry

He's a thief without a conscience, and he has gained skill with age. "He used to beg, but discovered that with patience and stealth his efforts were more productive," says brewery owner Jeff. "When he begged, people could see him. He learned that if he waited, and waited he could quietly sneak in and score the big loot when no one was looking." Steaks, lamb chops, and roasts are part of his larcenous booty. When Jeff adopted him from the Boulder County Humane Society 10 years ago, he needed to name him. "Phil the Dog was the first name that popped into my head," says Jeff, ". . . it fits him pretty well."

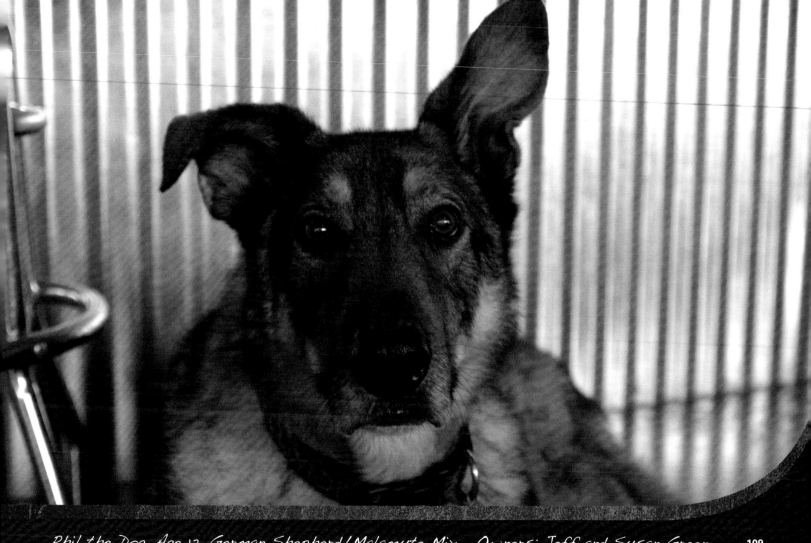

Phil the Dog, Age 12, German Shepherd/Malamute Mix   Owners: Jeff and Susan Green

Baxter

Founded 2009

Only branded brewpub without a brewpub

Promoter of: "Dogs, Beer, Colorado...it doesn't get much better!"

"**He gets the paper every morning.** If you forget, Baxter reminds you that he has a job to do," says publisher Brian Bennett. "It's especially great on a cold, snowy morning." At mealtime he picks up his food dish, prances it around the room a couple of times and drops it at your feet. He's an instinctive upland game dog, a flusher that always works out front, nose down, tail wagging. This can be a problem at home when you want to go down the stairs and he rushes past to go first. He's the "kiss cop and dance patrol" and will bark incessantly if anyone tries either illegal activity in front of him! "Even at ten, his fur is as soft as a puppy's. He's as snuggly as a bunny," says Becky Bennett, co-owner, publisher.

Baxter

Best Catch: He snagged a harassing Magpie right out of mid air

Most Annoying Habit: Drinks out of the toilet, then wants to say, "Hi!"

Most Excellent Adventure: Chasing seagulls on Oregon Coast beaches

Baxter, Age 10, English Springer Spaniel   Owners: Brian and Becky Bennett

Appendix

...COLORADO, IT DOESN'T GET MUCH BETTER

MORE BREWDOGS

MEET THE TEAM

Outtakes...too fun not to share!

Girls of Ska: Melissa Dunn – Sprocket (Boston Terrier),
Shannon Dillard – Foxy Cleopatra (Yorkie), Karen Muraro –
Otis (Aussie Shepherd), Cara Chama (German Shepherd)

Trinity BrewDogs: Tom Brown – Sage &
Deacon (2 Aussies), Johannah Murphy –
Cletus Hercules, Kurt – Tiger

Palisade BrewDogs Dan Brennan – Zeus (Black German Shepherd), Danny Wilson – Cash (Basenji/Shepherd Mix), Danny Wilson – Maggie (Mutt, Brown herding type), Dan Roos – Lexi (Black on White Aussie), Alexandra Sate – Koda (Chocolate Lab)

(Left to right) Cahoots, Josh Leeman, Paul Breaux, Luna (Pug), Pearl, Corkie Odell, Lauren Breaux, Helmut, Matt Jaspers, Cindy Loo

The Brew Fest

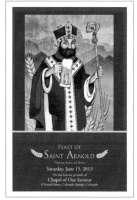

For any beer enthusiast a trip to Colorado should include a visit to a beer, or "brew" festival. This is where Colorado's craft brewers can introduce their products and their brands to an increasingly discerning public. Charities are major beneficiaries, because Colorado's liquor laws require that these special events have a charitable purpose. In most cases an admission fee will allow the patron to unlimited one to two ounce samples from between 20 and 50 breweries over a four to five hour period. Live music is generally an attraction with local and in some cases national headliners performing. Enriching the music and beer experience are a variety of food and craft vendors.

The publishers of this book have been a frequent part of the "enrichment experience" as The BrewDogs of Colorado. The mountain towns in summertime are excellent hosts. The natural beauty of the Rockies provide spectacular backdrops for great summer celebrations. The BrewDogs have enjoyed these parties in Breckenridge, Keystone, Winter Park, and Edwards, all ski towns. On the front range great events are hosted in Fort Collins, Loveland, Denver, Colorado Springs and Manitou Springs throughout the summer.

Plan your summer around a Colorado brew fest. Check the blogs for the calendar. If you like great beer and enjoy a fun outdoor party with a couple thousand other enthusiasts then get ready for a great summer in Colorado. ~ Cheers~

Great American Beer Festival

The Great American Beer Festival (GABF) is the premier beer festival in the United States. This event, produced by the industry's trade group, the Brewer's Association, puts Colorado and its beers on a national stage. At the GABF America's beer industry is strutting its stuff to the world, hosting breweries from all over the country. Demand for tickets has consistently exceeded supply with over 40,000 paid admissions attending four 4-hour sessions over three days.

Brewers regard this event as their chance to showcase their beers to an audience that is truly global. In 2013, beers were judged in 138 styles and 84 categories and subcategories, plus a pro-am competition. Over 4,000 beers are judged from over 600 U.S. breweries. Only three medals are awarded for each style; Gold, Silver, and Bronze. Clearly a GABF medal is a VERY BIG DEAL. A medal, any medal, will attract customers from all over the world. Many small breweries have literally become tourist destinations by winning a single GABF Medal.

Those lucky enough to be able to attend the event share in a truly unique experience. Imagine a party with 10,000 beer lovers trying to sample from 3,000 beers, one ounce at a time. With bagpipers on parade, characters in costume, and being a part of the beer industry's biggest trade show this event should be on every craft beer fan's bucket list.

To the Rescue

In Colorado, there are nearly 250* animal shelter and rescue groups. While some are professionally managed and staffed most are supported by passionate and caring volunteers reaching out to help unwanted, abused, abandoned, and homeless animals. These groups range from well established institutions to stand alone volunteer groups working in a particular service niche. They all need to raise funds and their events range from dog walks to dinners.

Over the past four years, we have been involved with festivals and events around the state of Colorado and when approached with requests, or have seen certain needs, we have willingly provided help through cash and in-kind donations to many of these deserving organizations. Many are mentioned below.

On the front range we have enjoyed participating as vendors in the Furry Scurry for the past four years. Sponsored by the Denver Dumb Friends League, the Furry Scurry is the country's largest Dog Walk, with over 12,000 people and 5,000 dogs participating. This two mile walk in Denver's Washington Park on the first Saturday in May is the League's largest single fund raiser, raising approximately $1,000,000. This event is really a giant dog party.

The established institutional organizations like the local humane societies or the Denver Dumb Friends League come immediately to mind. They provide shelter housing, adoption and other animal services in their communities. .

In the past years Colorado has been ravaged by wildfires, and recently flooding. The humane societies have been called upon as the first responders to provide shelter for the pets of displaced families. These events put extreme stress on the resources of these groups as pets arrive for shelter. Food becomes an immediate need. In 2012 during the summer festival season, The BrewDogs of Colorado were happy to donate a portion of their festival book sales sending cash donations to Larimer, Weld, Boulder, Pikes Peak and Grand County Pet Pals for dog food.

Rescue organizations such as National Mill Dog Rescue, and breed specific rescue groups actually seek out animals in abusive or cruel situations and attempt to "rescue" them. They then work to place them in safe, caring family situations. Many of these abuses occur in "puppy mills" where dogs are caged their entire lives and whose sole purpose is to birth puppies for retail sale in pet shops. In this edition Suzu (Very Nice Brewing) and Harley (City Star Brewing) were in these circumstances and are now experiencing life outside a cage for the first time. Make a point to read their stories.

Other groups focus on special situations. Safe Place for Pets, in Colorado Springs is a local grass roots volunteer organization that provides foster care and seeks to place pets that belonged to elderly citizens who had died, or could no longer care for their pets.

Another group, All Breed Dog Rescue and Training, focuses on hard to place dogs that are either, too large, or old, or that have had adjustment problems. Their services include foster parenting to re-socialize the dog, and placement. We partnered with Rockbottom Brewing in a fund raiser in 2010.

The vast majority of the dogs in this edition have been adopted or rescued. Many of our brewer partners are actively involved with these organizations as foster families and help raise funds. We are glad to be a part of this important community of caring people. We will continue to support them financially whenever we can. We believe in the work that they do.

Woof!))) Media, LLC
dba The BrewDogs of Colorado
publishers of:
The BrewDogs of Colorado
The BrewDogs of Colorado II

*source www. petfinders.com

In Memoriam

A tribute to those BrewDogs from the Original BrewDogs of Colorado that we have learned are no longer with us. Thanks for sharing your lives with us.

Poppy

Kaley

Kahlua

Angus

Chumley

Bruno

Bear

Reilly

135

Brewer

Chi

Zack

Camden

Harvey

George

Daisy

Jack

Meet the Team

Becky and Brian Bennett

Becky and Brian are the co-authors of both *The BrewDogs of Colorado*, and *The BrewDogs of Colorado II*, and co-founders of the publisher, Woof!))) Media, LLC. Since the original publication, they have managed and grown their merchandising and marketing company based on their ADDY award winning BrewDogs logo. This includes a popular merchandise line which is marketed on-line and at beer festivals around Colorado.

Lauren Olson

Lauren once again played a major role with the second edition of our book. Over the past few years she has maintained a constant presence in the craft brewing community. Her roles as Community Relations Manager at Bristol Brewing Company and founding member of Woof Media LLC!)) have yielded tremendous experience in the areas of marketing, sales, public relations and event coordination.

In *The BrewDogs of Colorado II*, Lauren cultivated and sustained relationships with the represented breweries and acted as a main point of contact throughout the project. She was the lead photographer for several spreads, consulted on creative design of the book and will continue to play an integral role in brand promotion.

Kristen Olson

Kristen launched the project in May by organizing the first contacts with brewers and initiating the strategic plan to execute the project. She also traveled and photographed several brewers and their dogs along the Colorado Front Range and managed the photography internship program that incorporated the works of Tory Rust. Her contributed efforts in social media, t-shirt design, and festival planning have been instrumental in the brand development over the years. Kristen resides in Colorado Springs with her 4-year-old son, and is employed at Bristol Brewing Company.

Photo Credits:

We appreciated all the contributors to this effort. This project could not have been completed without our photographers. In addition to the authors and members of the publishing group, our photo intern, Tory Rust, who is finishing her degree at the University of Denver contributed her considerable photo skills to the project.

Thank you to Evan Simon for the photo of Governor John Hickenlooper.

The flooding disasters that Colorado experienced in the late summer forced us to be flexible. Fortunately we were able to engage contributors who shared their photos with us. Estes Park Brewing Company photos by Lucian Oprea. Photos City Star's Harley are by Emily Wagner, Emily Sierra Photography.

Several photo shoots were team efforts so those will be acknowledged together.

Tory Rust: Caution, Black Bottle, Copper Kettle Brewing Company, Crooked Stave, Elk Mountain Brewing, Grimm

Brothers, Hall, High Hops Brewery, Odell (Pearl, and Cindy Loo), Verboten

Kristen Olson and Tory Rust: Dry Dock (Betty and Burton), Lone Tree, and Renegade

Kristen Olson: Boulder Beer, Equinox, Gravity, Rocky Mountain Brewery, Trinity (Tiger)

Lauren Olson: Bristol (Otis), Loveland Aleworks, Trinity (Sage and Deacon), Asher

Kristen Olson and Lauren Olson: Bristol (Pearl), Trinity (Cletus Hercules)

Becky Bennett: Aspen, BrewDogs, Crazy Mountain, Dry Dock (Schneider Clowder), Left Hand, Oskar Blues, Palisade, San Luis Valley, Ska, Telluride, Three Barrel, Very Nice

Brian Bennett: Odell (Cahoots)

*Please remember to support your local
animal rescue organizations.*